Walking in Switzerland's Berner Oberland

Easy Hikes in the Jungfrau Region

By Laurel L. Barton
and Richard G. Barton

3rd Edition

www.ProjectEasyHiker.com

Copyright ©ProjectEasyHiker 2023

All rights reserved. No part of this book may be reproduced in any form without written permission of the authors.

Third Edition 2023
Second Edition 2022
First Edition 2020

ISBN: 9798373651578

All photographs are by the authors. Reuse is prohibited without the express permission of the authors.

Advice to Readers

We have made every effort to ensure the accuracy of this book; However, changes can occur during the lifetime of an edition. As we are made aware of changes, they will be shown in the Updates section at our website www.ProjectEasyHiker.com. Please check for updates before your trip and also check locally with the Tourist Information Office for current transportation and trail conditions.

If during your trip you note changes, please submit them by email to ProjectEasyHiker@gmail.com.

Warning

Hiking and walking in the mountains can be dangerous. There is always a risk of personal injury or even death. Undertake this activity with a full understanding of the potential risks. While every effort has been taken for accuracy in the preparation of this guide, the user should be aware that conditions are highly variable. Weather can change in an instant affecting trail conditions and making a mountain walk, no matter how easy, more challenging and even dangerous.

Therefore, neither Project Easy Hiker, LLC, nor the authors, accept any liability for damage of any nature, including damage to property, personal injury, or death, arising from the information contained in this book.

Emergency assistance can be reached by dialing 144 on any available network.

Free to download, my144 is an App for all users of the iPhone. Should you require the emergency services, all you have to do is press the red button which connects you directly to the 144 emergency services. At the same time, it transmits your present GPS coordinates, enabling the emergency personnel to pinpoint your exact location.

Contents

PREFACE 1

HOW TO USE THIS GUIDE 3
    MAPS 3
    WALKING SPEED, DURATION, and DIFFICULTY 4
    TYPE OF HIKE 4
    WHAT TO CARRY 5

HIKES BY LOCATION AND CHARACTERISTICS 7

HIKES 9
    Hike #1 -- Grütschalp to Mürren 9
    Hike #2 – Lauterbrunnen Valley Walk 13
    Hike #3 – First to Grosse Scheidegg 17
    Hike #4 – First to Bachalpsee 23
    Hike #5 – Allmendhubel to Winteregg 27
    Hike #6 – North Face Trail 31
    Hike #7 – Kleine Scheidegg to Wengernalp 35
    Hike #8 – Männlichen to Kleine Scheidegg 39
    Hike #9 – Mönchblick Walk 45
    Hike #10 – Staubbachbänkli Walk 49
    Hike #11 – Iseltwald to Giessbach Falls 53
    Hike #12 – Thun Castle Walk 59
    Hike #13 – Aare Gorge (Aareschlucht) 65
    Hike #14 – Sagiweg 69
    Hike #15 – Stechelberg Loop 75
    Hike #16 – Lauterbrunnen to Zweilütschinen 79
    Hike #17 – Zweilütschinen to Wilderswil 83
    Hike #18 – Oeschinensee Trail to Lake 87
    Hike #19 – Sunnbüel-Arvenseeli 91
    Hike #20 – Lötschberger Nordrampe: Kandersteg to Blausee 95
    Hike #21 – Bussalp to Bort 99

OTHER EXCURSIONS 105
    Sulwald and Isenfluh 105
    Ballenberg, Swiss Open Air Museum 106
    Interlaken 107
    Bern 107

The Schilthorn and the Jungfraujoch 107
RAINY DAY IDEAS **111**
TRAVEL ADVICE **115**
　WHEN TO TRAVEL 115
　SAMPLE ITINERARIES.. 117
　HOW TO ARRIVE 119
　PASSES and TRANSPORTATION PLANNING 121
　Guidelines for selecting the right passes 122
　Transportation Planning.. 123

PREFACE

Three mountain view above Mürren, Hike #5

Our first trip to the Berner Oberland, specifically the Jungfrau Region, was in winter. We were in awe of the Swiss ability to keep walking trails groomed for *winter wandern* even as ski season was in full swing. The little mountain trains and the dramatic lifts captivated us, and we vowed to return in a snowless season.

We've now spent many weeks in the area delving deeper into the Jungfrau Region and greater Berner Oberland. Lauterbrunnen is our preferred base as it conveniently affords access to both the Wengen and Mürren sides of the valley but the villages at higher elevation have their own charm as well as pros and cons.

In writing this guide our goal is to share this unique spot with people who have time to savor it. If you love the outdoors and in particular hiking, ideally you would spend a week or more getting to know all the area has to offer and taking some side trips as well. If you only have three nights, you will still find it a fulfilling retreat on your longer European tour.

This book is for people who like to walk, who like to be in nature, but may not have the stamina for hiking all day. It is for seniors, people with children, and anyone who wants to experience the mountains but not climb them.

No car is required thanks to the Swiss system of interconnecting trains, buses, lifts, and ferries. Trails are groomed and well-signed, and the locals are multi-lingual. If you speak German, great! If not, English is widely spoken as the region welcomes tourists from all over the globe.

If you are planning a visit, you will find particulars on places to eat along the trail, how to take the trains, buses, and lifts, and most importantly, detailed directions on walks we have enjoyed over our years of travel to the Jungfrau Region.

All walks assume you are staying in Lauterbrunnen. If you have chosen to stay in one of the other villages or even more remotely it will be easy to figure out how to get to the starting point.

Before you go, check for updates on our website, **www.ProjectEasyHiker.com**. If you encounter any problems, please let us know by email **ProjectEasyHiker@gmail.com**.

Gute Reise!

Laurel & Richard Barton
February, 2023

P.S. – If you travel to Northern Italy's Dolomites, be certain to look for our book ***Walking in Italy's Val Gardena***. Connect with us on our blog, **www.Girovaga.com**, where we share updates from our travels, or on our Facebook page, **Project Easy Hiker**.

HOW TO USE THIS GUIDE

There is a plethora of information available online: So much that it can be challenging to sort through. This book presents some of the sources and information we have found most useful.

MAPS

The maps provide an overview of the route but the linked maps at www.PlotaRoute.com will allow you to zoom in on sections and see specific features. You can also change the view from the Standard Street Map that is pictured in the book to other views such as Terrain or Satellite views. The elevation profile of the route is shown in the online version where you can adjust a timer feature to suit your pace, get a weather forecast, and more. Play with it!

While maps are featured for each hike and links to the online maps are also included, a paper map is very useful as you may not have access to the internet when you need it. Stylized maps, which present a good overview of some trails, are available from the Tourist Information Offices (and online) but they are not suitable for way-finding if you get turned around or simply want to explore further. We recommend the map **"Lauterbrunnen Valley"** by **editionmpa** (see **bit.ly/LauterbrunnenMap**) available locally if you don't care to order it online. We also find using a map application on a smartphone helpful especially when reaching an unsigned road, looking for a bus stop, or seeking a café.

Travel times to-and-from trailheads can be deceiving and sometimes up to 90 minutes each way. Where possible, we have noted unusually long transit times from Lauterbrunnen, such as making a trip to the neighboring valley and the hikes at Kandersteg. When planning your day use the **SBB app** (see **bit.ly/SBBplanning**) -- available for Android and iPhone -- to check transit times.

WALKING SPEED, DURATION, and DIFFICULTY

This book references the length of each walk in terms of walking time. The kilometers and miles are also included.

We are not the slowest people on most trails we hike, but we are far from the fastest. It took several visits to realize that the signs that indicate how long it might take to get to the next junction/town/hut was an estimate based on a speed we do not usually maintain these days.

Although all of the walks are "easy," this book uses a scale of 1 to 3 as a further guide.

1. **Promenade** – Paved or partly paved and mostly level; well-signed and generally suitable for baby carriages.
2. **Easy hike** – Unpaved, crossing hills or mountain terrain, some ups and downs, or may have minimal signage.
3. **Extra Energy** – More exertion required due to length or extended uphill segments; may have loose gravel or moderately tricky footing.

TYPE OF HIKE

There are three types of hikes in this book.

1. **Out-and-Back:** Starts and ends at the same location; a round trip on the same path from where you set off walking.
2. **One-Way:** No need to turn around and hike back. Each one-way hike includes directions via public transportation.
3. **Loop:** A circuit that brings you back to the starting location. May also be a Lollipop where the "stem" is the same out and back.

WHAT TO CARRY

Although these are short treks, carrying along some basic supplies is advisable. Even if you plan to eat and refresh yourself at a mountain restaurant, water, snacks, and a jacket may come in handy.

Here is what we carry in our daypacks on each walk, no matter the duration.

- A rain-resistant jacket with hood and/or an additional warm layer
- Water (at least ½ liter each)
- Snacks such as trail mix, nuts, granola-type bars, fruit
- First aid supplies including a few bandages, small packets of antibiotic ointment, Benadryl Gel for bites, Advil, Tylenol, and Benadryl tablets as well
- Wet wipes for hygienic use
- Tissues
- Small bags, handy for debris (pack-it-in/pack-it-out)

These guys may mess up the trail, but you should pack-it-in, pack-it-out. Cow Parade, Lauterbrunnen, September.

HIKES BY LOCATION AND CHARACTERISTICS

Hike #	Name	Duration	Distance in Miles/Km	Difficulty
1	Grütschalp to Mürren	1H20M	2.8/4.5	1
2	Lauterbrunnen Valley Walk	2H	4.4/7.1	1
3	First to Grosse Scheidegg (2 versions)	1H45M to 2H	3.3/5.6 3.7/5.9	1 3
4	First to Bachalpsee	2H	4.1/6.6	2
5	Allmendhubel to Winteregg	1H30M	2.5/4.0	2
6	North Face Trail	2H	3.6/5.8	2
7	Kleine Scheidegg to Wengernalp	35M	1.4/2.3	1
8	Männlichen to Kleine Scheidegg	1H30M	2.9/4.7	2
9	Mönchblick Walk	1H	2.1/3.3	2
10	Staubbachbänkli Walk	1H	2.5/4.0	1
11	Iseltwald to Giessbach Falls	1H30M	3.3/5.2	2
12	Thun Castle Walk	2H	4.1/6.6	2
13	Aare Gorge	1H	1.5/2.3	2
14	Sagiweg	1H50M	3.4/5.5	2
15	Stechelberg Loop	50M	1.7/2.7	2
16	Lauterbrunnen to Zweilütschinen	1H20M	2.7/4.3	2
17	Zweilütschinen to Wilderswil	1H30M	3.1/5.0	1
18	Oeschinensee Trail to Lake	1H5M	2.4/3.8	2
19	Sunnbüel-Arvenseeli	2H	3.4/5.5	3
20	Lötschberger Nordrampe	1H30M	3.2/5.2	1
21	Bussalp to Bort	2H15M 1H50M	4.6/7.5 3.8/6.0	2

HIKES

Hike #1 -- Grütschalp to Mürren

Start:	Lauterbrunnen
End:	Mürren
Duration:	1H20M
Difficulty:	1
Distance:	2.8 miles/4.5 kilometers
Ascent/Descent:	721 feet ascent/229 feet descent
Type of Hike:	One-Way, return by public transportation
Transportation:	Gondola to Grütschalp from Lauterbrunnen; Gondola from Mürren to Stechelberg, Post Bus to Lauterbrunnen
Refreshments:	Lauterbrunnen village, Grütschalp mountain station, Winteregg, and Mürren village
WCs:	Same as Refreshments
Hiking Boots?	Sturdy shoes
Trekking Poles?	Optional

Walking toward Mürren just above the train track.

When we first visited the Jungfrau Region it was in winter, searching for some **winter wandern** or snow hiking. Our first hike that trip was from Grütschalp to Mürren. Now it is our traditional first-day hike in any season. The trail is easy, it takes less than 90 minutes, and the little town of Mürren offers great opportunities for sustenance be it lunch or simply a snack. Plus, there are optional additional hikes and touring to do by foot or by lift out of Mürren.

Paraglider above Mürren.

Starting in Lauterbrunnen, take the gondola to Grütschalp. Most of your fellow travelers will board the little vintage train for a quick ride to Mürren. This is clearly the thing to do if you are, by any chance, sleeping in Mürren and thus burdened with luggage.

Take some time to enjoy the view of the three peaks before seeking the trail that enters the woods just beyond the train station. There is a café here above the station where the trail starts. Do not walk along the tracks. Note the signage at the start of the hike. This is also the way to-or-from the Mountain View Trail which is a little higher, longer, and more difficult than the route described here.

This well-groomed path (even in winter) meanders through the woods with gentle ups-and-downs, frequently in sight of the train tracks and the little train chugging along with its baggage cart. Soon you arrive at Winteregg, roughly the halfway point and the terminus of a ski run in winter, with a restaurant and an intermediate stop for the train. Continue on with intermittent views of the mountains, now on a mostly flat trail following the tracks. The trail is still largely forested and will take you a final 40 minutes-or-so to Mürren. Wander through the town. Perhaps make a stop at Café Liv for *cappuccino* and a pastry or move on to the beautiful deck at Hotel Alpenruh for lunch with a view.

Satiated and refreshed, you are faced with several options. Nice weather might call you to venture to Piz Gloria on the Schilthornbahn. You can take the funicular from to Almendhubel to enjoy further hiking **(See Hikes #5 and #6)** if you still have the energy.

Another option is to walk down to cute little Gimmelwald (20 minutes), past perfectly-maintained Swiss houses with neat gardens and fat rabbits. Gimmelwald is a Rick Steves' favorite and worth a walk-through to see what a tiny mountain village is like. There are limited options for dining and sleeping but it is quaint and reminiscent of a simpler time. At Gimmelwald, one can take a dramatic gondola to the valley floor where the yellow Swiss Post Bus arrives promptly for a short ride back to Lauterbrunnen. Or you can take a peaceful walk through the **valley (See Hike #2)**, stopping at Trümmelbach Mürren Falls and pausing to watch base jumpers hurl themselves from the cliffs with their colorful parachutes.

No special equipment is required for this hike. Sturdy shoes, yes, with hiking boots and trekking poles optional (we always take ours). As always, prepare for the changeable weather in the mountains. Carry a jacket even if the day starts out warm, and water and snacks should be in your daypack.

The path to Mürren after an early September snow.

For an interactive map and elevation profile, visit
https://www.plotaroute.com/route/957025.

Hike #2 – Lauterbrunnen Valley Walk

Start:	Stechelberg
End:	Lauterbrunnen Bahnhof
Duration:	2H
Difficulty:	1
Distance:	4.4 miles/7.1 kilometers
Ascent/Descent:	232 feet ascent/567 feet descent
Type of Hike:	One-Way, with public transportation out-bound
Transportation:	Post Bus to Hotel Stechelberg
Refreshments:	Hotel Stechelberg, Weidstübli at Camping Jungfrau, Trümmelbach Falls
WCs:	Hotel Stechelberg, Gondola Lift Station Stechelberg, Camping Jungfrau, Trümmelbach Falls
Hiking Boots?	Sturdy shoes
Trekking Poles?	Not needed

The path through the valley.

On a cloudy – or even rainy day – this is nice option. Of course, it is even more stunning on a sunny day. Waterfalls spout out of the cliffs throughout the valley and rain only makes them more prominent. The entire route is mostly-downhill and suitable for small children and even prams.

We like to ride the Post Bus all the way to the Hotel Stechelberg and wander through the peaceful little town. Lovely gardens, avalanche shelters and a side trip to a waterfall await. **HINT**: download the **SBB app** (see **bit.ly/SBBplanning**) to your smart phone for all train and bus tickets, schedules, and planning.

From the bus stop, head south (further into the valley) and pass the hotel, veering left at a crossroads which is signed for Selfinenfall. Past a small utility building, cross the arched bridge to a viewing point for Selfinenfall, which may be rather modest if the season is dry. From here, retrace your steps to the bus stop and proceed north. (Alternatively, after viewing the falls you can cross the bridge over the Selfinen Lütschine and follow the path on the other side of the stream. View the map below online to more clearly see this optional detour.) Watch for paragliders and base jumpers as they sail above and into the valley in all sorts of weather.

Avalanche shelter

As you pass through Stechelberg note the decorated avalanche shelters. They look like sturdy bus shelters built by someone with a sense of humor, but they are lifesaving options should winter snows bring danger to the valley.

At the base station of the gondola, as you are walking toward Lauterbrunnen, turn left and find a small bridge across the stream, leading to a quiet path where you turn right heading to Lauterbrunnen. Now you are away from all traffic. Even as you rejoin a paved road, traffic is limited to locals-only until you get closer to Lauterbrunnen.

A little over 2 miles into the walk you can make a detour to view **Trümmelbach Falls**. The falls make a dramatic tumble inside of the mountain. You access the top of the falls via elevator then make your way down using stairs that allow you to see the powerful flow. If you choose this option, turn right to cross the bridge near Camping Breithorn, then left onto the shoulder of main road (watch out for traffic as the buses pass by and the road is narrow), reaching the entrance to the falls. After your tour, you can take the Post Bus back to Lauterbrunnen or rejoin the walk. To rejoin the walk, turn right out of Trümmelbach Falls and re-enter the trail network opposite the parking lot. Following the trails, re-cross the river on a foot bridge and soon rejoin the road you were traveling. You'll miss less than a mile of the original walk rejoining the road just before the 3rd mile. Zoom in on the online map to see details.

Transhumance valley style. A farmer moves his cows to the valley pasture in October by trailer.

On this walk you will pass farms with cows, sheep, and goats, as well as gardens and campgrounds. There is a vending machine with cheese, wine, and other food products along the route to fuel your picnic. Pick up a piece of fresh mountain cheese. You can't buy this at home!

Staubbach Falls is just outside of Lauterbrunnen and can be a nice rest stop or detour. The walk ends in Lauterbrunnen at the train station. As you pass through Lauterbrunnen there are many good choices for lunch or a snack. We like the **Airtime Café** for a light bite.

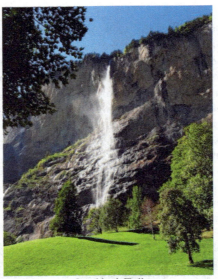
Staubbach Falls

For an interactive map and elevation profile, as well as the alternate route, visit **https://www.plotaroute.com/route/983430**

Hike #3 – First to Grosse Scheidegg

Start:	Grindelwald
End:	Grindelwald
Duration:	1H45M to 2H
Difficulty:	Panorama Trail: 1 Höhenweg: 3
Distance:	Panorama Trail: 3.3 miles/5.6 kilometers Höhenweg: 3.7 miles/5.9 kilometers
Ascent/Descent:	Panorama Trail: 334 feet ascent/1000 feet descent Höhenweg: 288 feet ascent/967 feet descent
Type of Hike:	One-Way, return by public transportation
Transportation:	Train to Grindelwald; Gondola to First; Post Bus from Grosse Scheidegg to Grindelwald
Refreshments:	Grindelwald restaurants, Berggasthaus First, Berghotel Grosse Scheidegg (summer only)
WCs:	Grindelwald, First gondola base station, Berggasthaus First
Hiking Boots?	Sturdy shoes for the Panorama Trail; Hiking boots for the Höhenweg
Trekking Poles?	Recommended

On the trail to Grosse Scheidegg

The trek from First (pronounced "feersht") to Grosse Scheidegg is magnificent. Usually, one would have to work much harder and deal with more people to have such stunning scenery. The adventure starts with a three-stage ride in the Grindelwald-First cable car, a 25-minute ride of more than 3 miles. Yes, another marvel of Swiss engineering. It is beautiful and it has been possible to take this ride since 1947. If all you have the energy to do is take the cable car, it is a worthy outing. But try to press on and you will be rewarded ten-fold!

From the top of the lift at First, there is also a hike to Bachalpsee. **(See Hike #4)** The hike to Grosse Scheidegg is far less crowded.

Grosse Scheidegg is the pass between Grindelwald and Meiringen. A bus makes the trip through the pass and is your easy-hiker return. More on that shortly. After your ascent, stop at the restaurant at the top of the gondola. We always start with a coffee and make use of the facilities. You can also watch the zip-liners on the "First Flyer" and take in the views from the **First Cliff Walk**.

The Panorama Trail: Way-finding is excellent as are the views.

The Panorama Trail as seen from the Höhenweg.

You have your choice of a truly easy route that is a pram-worthy road that is very easy to walk. We call this the Panorama Trail and rate it a "1" on our scale. The second route is more path than road and has some streams and rocky sections. This is the *Höhenweg*, a "3" on our scale. Both start at the top of the lift and each has fabulous views.

You will see nearly everyone heading left along a wide sweeping road. Where the trail splits, most people will go left to **Bachalpsee (Hike # 4)** but stay right following the curve of the road for this hike.

(FYI you can also take the alternative shortcut route noted on the map when you view it online, however, this shortcut is steeper and not a "1" on our scale.)

For the Panorama Trail, simply continue to follow signs to Grosse Scheidegg on a slightly undulating but generally downhill track wide enough for you to walk side-by-side. Enjoy views of the Schrekhorn, Wetterhorn and the mighty Eiger. Paragliders propel themselves off the cliffs sailing down to Grindelwald and providing delightful photo ops.

One of the authors on the Höhenweg.

If you are taking the *Höhenweg*, just after you complete the wide curve that starts both hikes, look for a sign that points to the left up a trail and is signed "Grosse Scheidegg." This path is part of the Eiger Ultra Trail and is a true hiking path. Despite the time indicated on the signs showing the Eiger option as 5 minutes faster, we found the Panorama Trail much easier. The *Höhenweg* has a couple of places where water will cross the trail if there's been rain or snow melt so it might be necessary to get your boots wet. Trekking sticks were imperative for us. Again, wayfinding is excellent so simply follow signs that variously say *Höhenweg*, Eiger Ultra Trail, and Grosse Scheidegg.

The Höhenweg can be rocky and crosses streams.

After about 3 miles, you will reach the hotel at **Grosse Scheidegg**. (It is closed in winter.) From late May until late October the bus to Grindelwald will stop here. Simply pay the driver on board if you do not have a pass. This is your easy-hiker, 25-minute way back to town. Make sure to check the bus departure times from Grosse Scheidegg as there is only one bus per hour to Grindelwald. See the schedule at **bit.ly/GrinBus.** Or you can hike back to First and take the lift down.

Panorama Trail – Difficulty 1

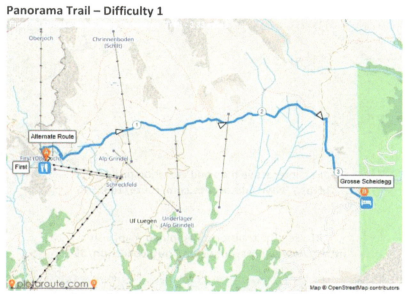

For an interactive map and elevation profile, visit
https://www.plotaroute.com/route/983381
and zoom in to see the alternate route for descent.

Höhenweg – Difficulty 3

For an interactive map and elevation profile, visit
https://www.plotaroute.com/route/1689595

To see the trails on a **combined** map, visit
https://www.plotaroute.com/routecollection/8342

You will see cows between May and late September.

Hike #4 – First to Bachalpsee

Start:	Grindelwald
End:	Grindelwald
Duration:	2H
Difficulty:	2
Distance:	4.1 miles/6.6 kilometers
Ascent/Descent:	734 feet ascent and descent
Type of Hike:	Out-and-Back
Transportation:	Train to Grindelwald; Gondola to First
Refreshments:	Grindelwald restaurants and Berggasthaus First
WCs:	Grindelwald; First gondola base station; Berggasthaus First
Hiking Boots?	Sturdy shoes
Trekking Poles?	Recommended

The lovely Bachalpsee, perfect for a picnic.

The trek from First (pronounced "feersht") to Bachalpsee is very popular for good reasons: it is reasonably easy and safe, and the destination is a perfect alpine lake. You will be in the company of many families as well as solitary hikers. The potential for a scenic picnic is excellent but in fine weather, expect crowds.

The First Cliff Walk

The adventure starts with a three-stage ride in the Grindelwald-First cable car, a 25-minute ride of more than 3 miles. Yes, another marvel of Swiss engineering. It is beautiful and it has been possible to take this ride since 1947. If all you have the energy to do is take the cable car, it is a worthy outing. After your ascent, stop at the restaurant at the top of the gondola. We always start with a coffee and make use of the facilities. You can also watch the zip-liners on the "First Flyer" and take in the views from the **First Cliff Walk**.

From the top of the lift or the restaurant, follow the easy signage and the well-trodden path. There is a rather steep start to this trail with about 400 feet of gain in the first three-quarters mile. The next mile-and-a-quarter are very slightly undulating and easy.

Typical landscape at high altitude on the way to the Bachalpsee.

We found the scenery reminiscent of some landscapes in Scotland: bare of trees but intensely green with interesting rock formations. Of course, Scotland does not have 13,000-foot mountains in the distance. You may pass cows grazing in the meadows (always fun) but don't disturb them, especially if they have calves.

Once you reach the lake take some time to savour the view, perhaps have a picnic. Return by the same path and take the lift back to Grindelwald. It is only because of the somewhat steep ascent and descent that we rated this hike a "2" on the Project Easy Hiker Scale. You might find hiking sticks helpful for the return descent.

From the top of the lift at First there is also a good one-way hike to Grosse Scheidegg **(See Hike #3)**, a less-crowded route than to Bachalpsee.

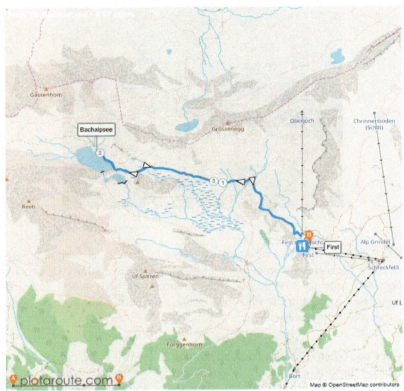

For an interactive map and elevation profile, visit
https://www.plotaroute.com/route/991444

Hike #5 – Allmendhubel to Winteregg

Start:	Mürren/Allmendhubel
End:	Winteregg
Duration:	1H30M
Difficulty:	2
Distance:	2.5 miles/4 kilometers
Ascent/Descent:	104 feet ascent/1112 feet descent
Type of Hike:	One-Way, return by public transportation
Transportation:	Train or gondola to Mürren then funicular to Allmendhubel; Return to Mürren by train or continue to Grütschalp by train and take the gondola to Lauterbrunnen
Refreshments:	Mürren, Allmendhubel, Winteregg
WCs:	Mürren, Allmendhubel, Winteregg
Hiking Boots?	Recommended
Trekking Poles?	Recommended

Playground at Allmendhubel with a 3-mountain backdrop.

This is an easier version of the Mountain View Trail which traverses the higher landscape between Mürren and Grütschalp. The Mountain View Trail is only about 3 miles long, but the descent is over 1799 feet versus 1112 on this easy-hiker version. Going to Winteregg is a knee-saver for us. This is a lovely afternoon hike as the sun will be behind you illuminating the mountains.

Make your way to Mürren via one of two routes:
- Gondola to Grütschalp and train to Mürren
- Bus to Stechelberg, two-stage gondola lift to Gimmelwald then Mürren

Once in Mürren, the funicular to **Allmendhubel** is your easy-hiker alternative to a steep uphill walk. At the top there is a restaurant and a terrific playground with amazing views. If you are towing children, you may never get to leave. There is also an alpine garden, which is a very easy path with in-season displays of mountain flora.

The author on the trail to Winteregg with a mountain view.

To walk to Winteregg, pass through the alpine garden either clockwise or anti-clockwise. Departing the alpine garden through a gate, paths lead both left and right. The left-hand trail is for **Hike #6, The North Face Trail**. To get to Winteregg, bear right and downhill. This portion is quite steep and trekking poles may be helpful.

Follow the marked Mountain View Trail turning off toward Oberberg (a farm) where the trail splits. The mountain views are spectacular as you cross meadows where cows graze in summer. On our mid-October hike, we encountered no cows and no other hikers although the afternoon was sunny and pleasant. There are some ups-and-downs, most particularly the long descending paved section after Oberberg (at 1805 meters). Then one gradually attains the woods while walking on a fairly substantial road to Winteregg.

Coming into Winteregg with its sunny terrace and Männlichen in the background.

If you are hungry, **Winteregg** would make a fine lunch stop on a sunny day with its fabulous terrace.

From Winteregg you have several choices to return to Lauterbrunnen:
- Train to Mürren and gondolas to Stechelberg with return by bus to Lauterbrunnen
- Train to Grütschalp and gondola to Lauterbrunnen
- Walk to Grütschalp on the lower trail **(see Hike #1)** then gondola to Lauterbrunnen
- Walk to Mürren on the lower trail **(see Hike #1)** then gondolas to Stechelberg and bus to Lauterbrunnen

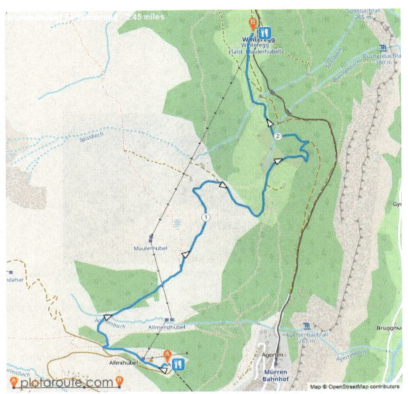

For an interactive map and elevation profile, visit
https://www.plotaroute.com/route/997171

Hike #6 – North Face Trail

Start:	Mürren/Allmendhubel
End:	Mürren
Duration:	2H
Difficulty:	3
Distance:	3.6 miles/5.8 kilometers
Ascent/Descent:	475 feet ascent/1332 feet descent
Type of Hike:	Loop
Transportation:	Train or gondola lift to Mürren then funicular to Allmendhubel; Return via train to Grütschalp or gondola to Stechelberg.
Refreshments:	Mürren, **Allmendhubel**, Sonnenberg, Suppenalp, **Schiltalp** (check hours locally for seasonal closures)
WCs:	Mürren, **Allmendhubel**, Sonnenberg, Suppenalp, **Schiltalp** (check hours locally for seasonal closures)
Hiking Boots?	Recommended
Trekking Poles?	Recommended

The view from the terrace at Schiltalp.

There are myriad variations on the North Face Trail with detours to the Sprutz waterfall, inclusion of Spielbodenalp, descent to Gimmelwald, and so on. We like this version which, at 2 hours, is just right for an easy hike and our knees are okay with the relatively modest descent. It is the descent that causes us to rate this a "3" on our easy-hiker scale. It is generally a gentle descent, but it is long. Mürren is the perfect endpoint offering many options for lunch and modes of transportation to return to your base.

As in **Hike #5**, make your way to Lauterbrunnen (or wherever your base may be) to Mürren via one of two routes:
- Gondola to Grütschalp and train to Mürren
- Bus to Stechelberg, two-stage gondola lift to Gimmelwald then Mürren

Once in Mürren, the funicular to **Allmendhubel** is your easy-hiker alternative to a steep uphill walk. At the top there is a restaurant and a terrific playground with amazing views. If you are towing children, you may never get to leave. There is also an alpine garden trail, which is a very easy walk with in-season displays of mountain flora.

The trail before it descends to Sonnenberg which is at the lower left. The Birg mountain lift station is on the peak.

Pass through the alpine garden area either clockwise or anti-clockwise as they end up at the same end-point. Departing the alpine garden area through a gate, paths lead both left and right. The right-hand trail is for **Hike #5,** so take the left-hand trail toward **Sonnenberg** also signed as the North Face Trail.

N.B. You can also go below the playground and follow the path around to the right through a light forest instead of going through the alpine garden.

The descent to Sonnenberg is a little steep but easy enough. As usual, we like to have our trekking poles for stability. Sonnenberg is early in the hike, but it is the best bet to be open for refreshments if you are outside of the mid-June to mid-September hiking season (we often go in late September). Sonnenberg is also open in the winter for skiers and those who do *winter wandern* (winter hiking on groomed trails).

Apple strudel at Schiltalp.

From Sonnenberg, follow the trail to **Suppenalp**, also a *pension*, then across meadows and past farms, making one last ascent through lightly forested land shortly before **Schiltalp**. These alps (cheese-making farms) may very well be closed outside of the high-summer season so check locally if you are counting on one for a rest stop. We can attest to the quality of the apple strudel at Schiltalp, made fresh daily!

After Schiltalp, the trail descends gradually, again past little huts and farms. You will see the lifts leading to Birg and the Schilthorn and always have fantastic views of the mountain peaks across the valley.

If desired, extend this hike by veering off to the Sprutz waterfall and **Spielbodenalp** (where there is a seasonal restaurant operating June through late September), well-marked by trail signs.

If a detour is not in your plans, continue on the main trail, which eventually becomes a road, to the hamlet of Gimmeln and on into Mürren where you will arrive near the Stechelberg/Gimmelwald gondola. The **Hotel Alpenruh** has a lovely terrace for a post-hike lunch.

For an interactive map and elevation profile, visit
https://www.plotaroute.com/route/998687

Hike #7 – Kleine Scheidegg to Wengernalp

Start:	Kleine Scheidegg
End:	Wengernalp
Duration:	35M
Difficulty:	1
Distance:	1.4 miles/2.3 kilometers
Ascent/Descent:	6 foot ascent/587 feet descent
Type of Hike:	One-Way, return by public transportation
Transportation:	Train to Kleine Scheidegg from either Grindelwald or Lauterbrunnen; Train from Wengernalp to Wengen and on to Lauterbrunnen
Refreshments:	Kleine Scheidegg
WCs:	Kleine Scheidegg
Hiking Boots?	Not necessary
Trekking Poles?	Not necessary

The Jungfraujoch train as viewed from this trail.

This is a super easy – almost <u>too</u> easy – walk. It is not long, it is not steep, there is no uphill, no rocks, no obstacles. For those who have hiked from Männlichen to Kleine Scheidegg **(Hike #8)**, this is a nice add-on if you are game for a little more mileage. This is not as strenuous as walking all the way to Wengen which is, to us, a knee-killer as the descent is considerable.

Why do we include it? The views are amazing, and it would be easy enough to push a pram or walk with very young children. It is a good leg-stretcher after the train ride down from the Jungfraujoch or up from Grindelwald or Wengen.

View along the trail to Wengernalp.

To take this walk, find the road/trail behind the station at Kleine Scheidegg. The signage is clear, pointing to Wengen and Wengernalp. The beginning of the hike yields fabulous views of the three mountains but particularly the Mönch and Jungfrau, as well as the little Jungfraujoch train. Further on, turning away from the full mountain view, traverse above the Lauterbrunnen Valley catching sight of Mürren in the distance. Cows peacefully graze here amazing close to steep cliffs. You'll also see the little train that runs up-and-down between Wengen and Kleine Scheidegg. In no time at all, you will reach the little station at Wengernalp.

Trains run every half-hour so you can return to Kleine Scheidegg or go down to Wengen and on to Lauterbrunnen.

By now you probably have experienced how well-connected the area is. This walk could be a segment on a round-trip tour from Lauterbrunnen or Grindelwald. For example:
- **Train from Lauterbrunnen to Wengen**
- **Gondola to** Männlichen
- Hike to Kleine Scheidegg **(Hike #8)**
- Have lunch
- Walk to Wengernalp
- Take the train to Lauterbrunnen

Or
- **Gondola from Grindelwald to** Männlichen
- Hike to Kleine Scheidegg **(Hike #8)**
- Have lunch
- Walk to Wengernalp
- Take the train to Lauterbrunnen and on to Grindelwald

For an interactive map and elevation profile, visit
https://www.plotaroute.com/route/1000117

Hike #8 – Männlichen to Kleine Scheidegg

Start:	Wengen
End:	Kleine Scheidegg
Duration:	1H30M
Difficulty:	2
Distance:	2.9 miles/4.7 kilometers
Ascent/Descent:	295 feet ascent/830 feet descent
Type of Hike:	One-Way, return by public transportation
Transportation:	Gondola to Männlichen from Wengen (or Grindelwald); Train back to Wengen or Grindelwald from Kleine Scheidegg
Refreshments:	Männlichen or Kleine Scheidegg for restaurants, or picnic stop half-way along the trail.
WCs:	Männlichen, Porta-Potty at picnic spot, Kleine Scheidegg
Hiking Boots?	Recommended
Trekking Poles?	Recommended

The view to the Grindelwald Valley from the trail.

We have seen young, old, and in-between on this trail. Yes, it can get busy as it seems like a favorite of most everyone. Somehow hikers spread out and, at least when we visit, it isn't so busy that there is a line-up on the trail. So, go!

Männlichen is a worthwhile trip even for non-hikers. The views are excellent, there is a restaurant, and for those with children a unique playground will keep them busy while you chill.

We show the start from Wengen, but one can start from Grindelwald as well. Just get yourself to **Männlichen** via one of the gondolas. The ride up from Wengen is dramatic with views of the Lauterbrunnen Valley, waterfalls, and the gondola to Grütschalp directly across. Sometimes you may see – or hear – marmots below the top station of the lift.

Massive cow containing a slide at the playground.

Stop in the restaurant for a pre-hike *cappuccino* and to use the facilities as there is only a chemical toilet along the route. The start of the walk is well-marked from the deck of the restaurant, past the playground.

The route proceeds in a generally downhill and gradual manner. There is a slight uphill at the 1 mile point and for about one-third of a mile. The last 2+ miles are downhill, a little steeper as you descend into Kleine Scheidegg. As such, we recommend hiking poles and boots.

Hiking in-and-out of sunlight, depending on the time of day, you will have a tremendous view of the mountains with the Eiger and the Wetterhorn, which soars over Grindelwald, particularly prominent during the first half of the hike. Mind your step if it has been cold. While the trail is well-maintained tiny puddles turn into skating rinks overnight if there has been rain. Do stay safely on the trail and avoid trampling the tender high alpine foliage as well as dangerous footing next to ledges. You will get great views from the trail.

The author at the rest stop.

About halfway, there is a popular viewpoint and picnic spot where we often encounter a dozen-or-so people enjoying the view and a rest. Here it is acceptable to leave the trail and lounge on the grass or on one of the few benches. There is also a chemical toilet, a rare find on a hiking trail. By now you are seeing the peak of the Jungfrau as well. Continuing your hike around a long, sweeping curve, you come at last to **Berghaus Grindelwaldblick** with a very inviting deck, perfect for a post-hike lunch if you've timed it well. But if it is too busy you are within sight of Kleine-Scheidegg and the restaurants there. The new **Restaurant Eigernordwand** has an amazing deck.

From Kleine Scheidegg you can
- Go up to the Jungfraujoch (reservations required so timing is crucial)
- Take the train to Wengen and on to Lauterbrunnen
- Take the train to Grindelwald

- Continue your hike by walking down to Wengernalp **(See Hike #7)**
- Hike back to Männlichen and take a gondola either to Wengen or Grindelwald

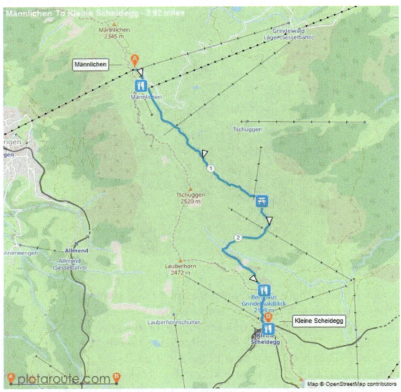

For an interactive map and elevation profile, visit
https://www.plotaroute.com/route/1000150

The Mönch and the Jungfrau viewed from the trail to Kleine Scheidegg

Hike #9 – Mönchblick Walk

Start:	Wengen train station
End:	Wengen church
Duration:	1H
Difficulty:	2
Distance:	2.1 miles/3.3 kilometers
Ascent/Descent:	423 feet ascent/403 feet descent
Type of Hike:	Lollipop Loop
Transportation:	Train to/from Wengen otherwise on foot
Refreshments:	Wengen village
WCs:	Wengen village
Hiking Boots?	Sturdy shoes
Trekking Poles?	Desirable

View to Lauterbrunnen from the Mönchblick on a cloudy day.

The Mönch can only be seen from one spot in Wengen and this is it. Even better, this is where you can enjoy a fabulous view of Lauterbrunnen, the valley, and Staubbach Falls. It is suitable for small children and even with prams. The Mönchblick (literally "Monk view") is a good choice any time: Morning for the light, evening as a leg stretcher after dinner (as long as there's daylight), even on a cloudy day when the entire view may not be clear. It is also a good choice when footing at higher elevations is treacherous after a snow.

This is an easy walk, however, we recommend sticks for added security on portions of the trail.

The Mönch as seen from the Mönchblick.

From the train station in Wengen, head up the main street, turning left onto the street in front of the imposing Palace Hotel. Take a sharp left after the Hotel Bellevue and descend to the tracks making a sharp right-hand turn paralleling the tracks, now on a path not a road. Soon you will reach Wengwald, a tiny station where the train stops only on demand. Notice it even has a ticket machine. The Swiss are serious about train service and collecting fares.

Follow the path to a **sharp left turn** where you rejoin the road just after the one-mile point. At the "T" turn left and find the Mönchblick at the end of the road.

This is one of the best views of the valley. Riding the train between Lauterbrunnen and Wengen you get glimpses of the valley with the town, its iconic church and Staubbach Falls but here you can enjoy the view as long as you like.

The view of the valley on a sunny day.

When you have soaked up the view, return via the road. At the "T" where you turned left to the Mönchblick, do not turn but continue on the road instead of taking the path back to Wengwald, looping above the outward-bound route and eventually rejoining your outbound route by the Hotel Bellevue. Across from the Palace Hotel, take the turn to the church for another good viewpoint, although not as lovely as the Mönchblick.

If you are pushing a pram or would rather walk only on a paved surface, it is certainly feasible to use the road as an out-and-back instead of looping down to Wengwald and the path.

Return to the train station for your return or onward journey.

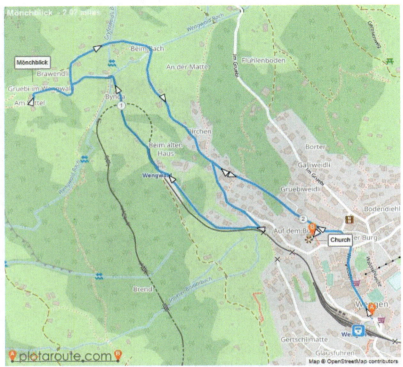

For an interactive map and elevation profile, visit
https://www.plotaroute.com/route/1000969

Hike #10 – Staubbachbänkli Walk

Start:	Wengen train station
End:	Wengen train station
Duration:	1H
Difficulty:	1
Distance:	2.5 miles/4 kilometers
Ascent/Descent:	295 feet ascent/295 descent
Type of Hike:	Out-and-Back
Transportation:	Train to/from Wengen otherwise on foot
Refreshments:	Wengen village
WCs:	Wengen village
Hiking Boots?	Not required
Trekking Poles?	Not required

Surrounded by mountains, the hike starts on a quiet road as Wengen is a car-free village.

Staubbachbänkli is just a tiny bit longer than the Mönchblick **(Hike #9) but equally delightful and very easy.**

Departing the train station, look for the Coop store across from which you will see the road that dips beneath the train tracks and enters an area of small hotels and houses. Keep left at the Hotel Baren. Note the local signage shows the route to **Staubbachbänkli** going both right and left. We suggest left as you stay on a road. To the right it becomes a path which eventually rejoins the road. Your choice!

Enjoy wide views of the valley and Mürren as well as private homes, gardens, and small farms. Very soon you arrive at **Staubbachbänkli** where a number of benches invite contemplation of the view. In December-May ibexes can, according to local sources, often be seen.

Return to Wengen by the same road or take an alternative path as desired. The link to our online map may inspire you to try one of the many trails that crisscross this area.

The view from the Staubbachbänkli

For an interactive map and elevation profile, visit
https://www.plotaroute.com/route/1002306

Hike #11 – Iseltwald to Giessbach Falls

Start:	Iseltwald
End:	Giessbach Falls
Duration:	1H30M
Difficulty:	2
Distance:	3.3 miles/5.2 kilometers
Ascent/Descent:	574 feet ascent/534 feet descent
Type of Hike:	One Way, return by public transportation
Transportation:	Train to Interlaken Ost; Bus to Iseltwald; Funicular (opt.) to Hotel Giessbach; Boat or Boat/Train combo to Interlaken Ost
Refreshments:	Iseltwald and Giessbach
WCs:	Iseltwald and Giessbach
Hiking Boots?	Recommended
Trekking Poles?	Recommended

Giessbach Falls

This is a lovely walk along Lake Brienz with frequent sightings of the ferries that ply the placid lake as well as views of the surrounding mountains. While this hike is a bit over three miles long, the elevation change is modest, less than 600 feet of gain and just over 500 feet of descent. Still, it is a good workout with the option of a steep climb at the end. Easy hikers make the final ascent via funicular...if you can time it right!

We did **not** time it right and missed the funicular by 5 minutes, necessitating an 18 minute trek up switchbacks. At least we didn't have to push a pram like one of our fellow wayfarers.

Make your way to Interlaken Ost, where the adventure begins. In the big plaza in front of the station you will find the bus #103 which will take you to the center of the little village of Iseltwald. From the bus stop, follow the road that curves along the lake, eventually becoming a path.

The route is not tricky: just stay on the path. The tricky part is timing as the funicular does not run often. No big deal if you are willing to make the climb at the end. Below is a recommended schedule for a walk with lunch at the top based on schedules for 2022 (see link below). Return options are explained at the end of this chapter.

Bus #103 from Interlaken Ost	Walk to base of funicular	Funicular Up	Funicular Down options	Ship/train back to Interlaken
dp 11:05 / ar 11:26	dp 11:30 / ar 13:00	13:14	13:40	13:51 (1)
			14:00	14:09 (2)
			14:40	14:51 (1)
			16:00	16:09 (2)

(1) To Interlaken Ost by ship
(2) To Brienz by ship/Change to train to Interlaken Ost

Note: The funicular schedule is subject to change and may vary in Spring, Summer, and Fall. There are many exceptions such as "only on Saturday" or "only when the group is large enough." Download the PDF for the current year and study it to make certain you know when it is operation and how much time you will have at the hotel. See **bit.ly/Fun2023** for the PDF.

You could also take the 9:05 bus and catch either the 11:14 or 11:54 funicular up to the hotel.

A tunnel on the trail.

As to the path, it undulates a bit with ever-changing views of the lake and mountains. It is quite level for first 25% with pavement then gravel, but eventually becoming a true trail with rocks, undulations, and tree roots. The last 20% is also fairly level.

There is a tunnel, a dramatic overhang, and a rustic picnic/rest area at the highest point of the route. This hike is well-shaded, lovely on a hot day. While the views from the trail are terrific, ahead lies the great waterfall at Giessbach and many trails to explore if you still have the energy!

A ferry on Lake Brienz, a good return option.

When you reach a point where the trail signs indicate you can go up or down to Hotel Giessbach, choose down*, as it leads to the funicular and boat station. Then shortly, when you come to stairs, choose the stairs down toward what looks like a shed. There is an old sign that says "Seilbahn" and points to the left. Make your way carefully down these stairs and pass through a short tunnel to the boat station, then up a ramp to the base of the funicular. CHF 5.00 one way, no discounts. CHF 10.00 per person roundtrip, CHF 8.00 with Berner Oberland Regional Pass. No discounts for Half Fare Card.

*You can certainly hike up to the hotel on the branch of the trail that heads uphill. We have not done it.

Looking over the driver's shoulder descending to the lake on the funicular.

If you wish to walk up the switchbacks (or have missed the funicular as we did), proceed past the funicular and boat stations following the path along the lake and over a bridge. The water here tumbles but the best is yet to come. Take the switchbacks up up up. After 18 minutes arrive at the hotel and the perfectly lovely Giessbach Falls, earning your lunch. Walking up the switchbacks turns this walk into a "3" on the Easy-Hiker Scale.

Whichever way you arrive, take a few moments to admire the views from the sizable terrace of the Grand Hotel Giessbach. In season, one can dine on the terrace, otherwise inside the Park Restaurant Les Cascades. The food is excellent, and the restaurant features old-fashioned high-end hospitality service (remember who runs the major hospitality schools) and prices that may make you blink, but it is perfectly acceptable to have lunch in your post-hike disheveled condition.

There is also a kiosk for takeaway meals, beverages, ice cream, and snacks. If you purchase a snack, you can relax on the terrace by the kiosk. We also saw people eating their packed sandwiches having purchased a beverage from the kiosk.

Lunch completed, you may wish to explore the hotel grounds further. When it is time to return to Interlaken Ost, take the funicular down to meet a ship. The funicular runs in synch with the ship schedule, so if you arrive as we suggest on the funicular at 13:14, have a look around and a leisurely lunch, you can take the funicular down at 16:00 and catch the ship to Brienz followed by the train to Interlaken Ost. The last ship varies by season so consult that online schedule if you wish to stay longer.

Lake Brienz view from the hotel

For an interactive map and elevation profile, visit
https://www.plotaroute.com/route/1003126

Hike #12 – Thun Castle Walk

Start:	Thun
End:	Oberhofen Castle
Duration:	2H
Difficulty:	2
Distance:	4.1 miles/6.6 kilometers
Ascent/Descent:	354 feet ascent/334 feet descent
Type of Hike:	One Way, return by public transportation
Transportation:	Train to Thun; Return via bus from Oberhofen to Thun or Interlaken or via boat to Thun then train to Interlaken
Refreshments:	Thun; Dampfschiff Restaurant; Hilterfingen; Oberhofen
WCs:	Thun; Dampfschiff Restaurant; Hilterfingen; Oberhofen
Hiking Boots?	Not necessary
Trekking Poles?	Not necessary

Castle and Thun viewed from the promenade along the lake.

NB: The trip to Thun from Lauterbrunnen is one hour one-way by train, so this outing is at least a half-day trip.

Thun (pronounced rather like "tune") is the big city of the Jungfrau Region at 43,000 people. It is very walkable, scenic, and a pleasant place to while away a day or, at least, the morning before heading off on your walk. There are many appealing cafes, stunning covered bridges, and a pedestrian-friendly center, not to mention the stunning Thun Castle dating to the 12th Century. Along the way you will see three more castles, ships plying the Thunersee, and the lovely Swiss mountains are ever in your sight.

The walk has little elevation gain overall, but some steeper inclines in the final third of the walk cause us to rate this walk a "2" on our scale.

Take the train to Thun Bahnhof from Lauterbrunnen via Interlaken Ost and Spiez. Exiting the station, walk up **Aarefeldstrasse** to the bridge over the Flusswelle Thun, where you may see people surfing! This is the Aare River which feeds both the Thunersee (Lake Thun) and Brienzersee (Lake Brienz) where you'll find **Hike #11**. The Aare River also features prominently in **Hike #13** where you can trek through a gorge at the far end of Lake Brienz.

After crossing the bridge, you are now on an island, follow **Freienhofgasse** with the river on your right on until you cross the covered bridge at **Untere Schleuse** coming out in the **Mühleplatz** with its many cafes.

NB: It may be helpful to use the link to the online maps, below, and zoom in on the detailed portions of this walk.

Thun Castle

Turn right into the underpass by El Camino Café and then left onto **Obere Hauptgasse**, following this street to **Rathausplatz** where you make a right turn and find your way to a significant staircase leading you up toward the castle. Consult our map as this area can be a bit confusing. Signage to the castle was not obvious during our visit. Once on the stairs, you achieve some altitude and come out in a path system around **Castle Thun**. Keep to your left and make your way up. The castle is open as a museum, but walkers can simply pass through and take in the views.

Alternatively, there is a shortcut via elevator that allows you to avoid the "significant staircase" mentioned above. From **Obere Hauptgasse** at #29 there is a passage to Schlossberg Parking. Take this tunnel and the elevator will carry you to the castle level. This is noted with a red-dashed line on the Plotaroute map (link below).

When you are ready to move along, exit the castle at the opposite end from that you entered and take the flight of stairs down to your right, exiting onto **Hohle Messe**. Follow **Hohle Messe** to another set of stairs down at **Kirchtreppe**, turning left at the bottom onto **Obere Hauptgasse** taking the first right onto **Freienhofgasse** leading to a bridge. Turn left before the bridge, onto **Aarequai** leading you along the lake. The hard part is over for a while as you stay on this promenade for over a mile, although it changes name a couple of times.

The Promenade along the lake.

A little past the one mile mark is a good restaurant, the **Dampfschiff**. Your next café option is not until past milepost 3 in **Hilterfingen**, so time it well if you plan on lunch during your walk. There are also end-of-walk options in **Oberhofen**. Continue along the lakeshore with mountain views and, across the lake, the **Schloss Schadau**, with a history dating back to 1348. It is now a hotel, restaurant, and events venue. When you reach the ferry landing at **Hunibach**, turn left past the playground then right onto **Alpenstrasse**. You could also board a passenger ship and take a lake cruise from here if you wish to truncate the walk.

Alpenstrasse leads you to **Staatsstrasse** which you will follow to a Y by a bus stop. Take the left-hand branch of the Y uphill on **Alte Thunstrasse** until you reach a park. Turn right at the first road into **Hüneggpark** arriving shortly at **Schloss Hünegg**. Follow one of the paths in the park to exit coming eventually to **Hüneggweg**. Now zigzag a bit (follow our map) until you reach **Dorfstrasse**, following it to a beautiful view over the village church and the highest point on this walk. Descend on **Schneckenbühlstrasse** taking a left onto **Staatsstrasse** arriving at **Schloss Oberhofen**, your 4th and final castle. Note many sites, including this castle, close seasonally and often on Mondays or holidays, so if touring one or more is essential, check details before you start the walk.

The alps as viewed from Thun.

Whew! After this walk you may want to relax on a ship going back to Thun or even to Spiez or Interlaken West where you can connect to a train back to Lauterbrunnen or wherever you are staying. Alternatively, buses #21 and #25 go back to the Thun Train Station (*Bahnhof*) from Staatsstrasse. You can buy tickets from a machine on board the bus but have change available. CHF 3.30 as of this writing. This bus is not covered by the Berner Oberland Regional Pass. As a reminder (See Chapter on Transportation) having the **SBB app** on your smartphone will be very helpful in determining your options.

For an interactive map and elevation profile, visit
https://www.plotaroute.com/route/1003863

For a close up of the castle area, visit
https://www.plotaroute.com/map/2115939

Hike #13 – Aare Gorge (Aareschlucht)

Start:	Aareschlucht Ost train stop
End:	Aareschlucht West train stop
Duration:	1H
Difficulty:	2
Distance:	1.5 miles/2.3 kilometers
Ascent/Descent:	449 feet ascent/633 feet descent
Type of Hike:	One Way
Transportation:	From Lauterbrunnen, train to Interlaken Ost, train to Meiringen, train to Aareschlucht Ost stop-on-demand; To return, Aareschlucht West train stop-on-demand to Meiringen, train to Interlaken Ost and train to Lauterbrunnen
Refreshments:	Restaurants at East and West entrances; Café du Pont at West entrance
WCs:	East and West entrances
Hiking Boots?	Not necessary
Trekking Poles?	Not necessary

Walkway through the Aare Gorge

Like **Hike #12**, this is a day trip beyond the Lauterbrunnen Valley and along the Aare River. The *Aareschlucht,* or Aare Gorge, is a natural wonder that the ingenious Swiss opened for walking in 1887. When you take this trek on elevated walkways and through tunnels, imagine the early tourists in their Victorian Era fashions discovering the gorge on newly built walkways, wooden in those days. **Prices and hours here**. Note that the gorge is closed during winter and early spring.

A narrow point in the gorge.

Our recommended starting point is the east entrance for the way the gorge reveals itself on the way west. Also, the path is mostly descending in this direction. (See the elevation graphic by using the link to the online map below.) The path is pram friendly only on the west end, so if traveling with a child in a stroller, start at the west end and plan to go only about halfway into the gorge then return to the west entrance.

Starting from Lauterbrunnen, your trip to the east entrance takes one-hour-18-minutes. Trains run about every half hour. The route is simply Lauterbrunnen to Interlaken Ost connecting to Meiringen and finally to Aareschlucht Ost MIB. The final train is a tiny local train almost like a trolley, and you must request the stop by pressing a button. Not to worry, others will most likely be exiting with you but do pay attention. It is a five minute ride from Meiringen to Aareschlucht Ost. Once you pass the Aareschlucht West stop, press the stop request button which may be labeled *Halt auf verlangen*.

It will look like you are being dropped off inside a tunnel but suddenly a door in the side of the tunnel will open opposite the train door. Exit and follow the path across the river then ascend (this is the only major ascent on the hike) 350 feet, first on wooded paths and eventually to a road. Turn right to the visitors' center and entrance. Here you will find restrooms and a snack bar, the last chance until the visitors' center on the far end, an hour's walk away.

Buy your tickets and descend on walkways (pictured) to the gorge. From here you have no choice in route: simply follow the walkways, passing through tunnels and some narrow (about 1 meter wide) passages here-and-there. The light changes constantly as the gorge narrows and widens. In some places the water surges and in others it is almost placid.

This is a good option any time, good weather or poor. If it is raining, you are partially protected and the views are just as good as in dry weather.

When you reach the end of the paths you are in the west visitors' center with a playground, restrooms, and a café. Exit and walk through the parking lot and down the road to a bridge. Across the bridge is the train stop and also a little café (closed Monday and Tuesday). From the VC to the train stop is a 6 or 7 minute walk. This is a stop-on-demand location so press the button. Trains run about every half hour.

Retrace your route to Lauterbrunnen via Meiringen and Interlaken Ost.

For an interactive map and elevation profile, visit
https://www.plotaroute.com/route/1005181

Hike #14 – Sagiweg

Start:	Gimmelwald Lift Station
End:	Gimmelwald Lift Station
Duration:	1H50M
Difficulty:	2
Distance:	3.4 miles/5.5 kilometers
Ascent/Descent:	700 feet descent/700 feet ascent
Type of Hike:	Lollipop
Transportation:	Post Bus to Stechelberg, Gondola to Gimmelwald. Alternately, lift from Grütschalp, train to Mürren, and gondola down to Gimmelwald.
Refreshments:	Limited in Gimmelwald
WCs:	Gimmelwald Lift Station and an outhouse near the sawmill
Hiking Boots?	Not required
Trekking Poles?	Optional

Gimmelwald is a charming non-commercial mountain village that reflects, to some degree, the "old" Switzerland before modernization and rampant tourism. Rick Steves favors the village as a place to stay although we find it too lacking in services and options for our purposes. Still, it is a delightfully quiet place to launch an easy hike. We rated this a "2" on the easy-hiker scale due to the uphill return, but it is otherwise very easy.

The "Sagiweg" is a circular tour including view onto the Lauterbrunnen Valley at Fluh, a bubbling stream, the Selfinen-Lütschine, and a traditional saw mill that is more than 160 years old and still runs on water power. We truncate the hike at Im Tal to keep the duration under two hours, but you could easily extend your expedition into this appealing valley. *Sägirei* means sawmill in German, so "Sagiweg" is roughly "path to the sawmill."

Most of this route is a wide road and easy to walk.

Whether you come up from Stechelberg on the gondola or down from Mürren, this walk begins at the Gimmelwald Lift Station. If you are traveling with children, you may need to stop at the compelling playground by the lift station. Otherwise, head straight up the road, passing Pension Gimmelwald and Ollie and Maria's B&B until you come to a sharp bend to the left marked as a junction to Im Tal. (**NB:** Some sources tell you to turn left at Pension Gimmelwald and take the downhill path. We found the footing challenging and prefer the easier route along the road, which is pram worthy.)

From the bend, follow this road – eventually it becomes a graveled road through the forest – downhill to the viewpoint over the Lauterbrunnen Valley. You can see all the way to Wengen. Continue downhill winding through farms, alongside the Selfinen-Lütschine river, arriving at an active 1858 sawmill in the Sefinen Valley.

The playground-with-a-view by the Gimmelwald lift station.

Approximately 10 minutes after the sawmill, there is a junction with another graveled road. This junction is the Im Tal Sefinental. There is a barbecue/picnic area along the river. Turning right will return you to Gimmelwald, our recommendation for an easy walk. Or you can extend your outing for a mile or two by proceeding forward. Be aware there are no services.

The return from Im Tal is uphill all the way, but fairly gentle. This route is always a road, paved or graveled, and never a path. Passing through the village you will see a couple of "honor stores" where gift items and souvenirs are displayed for your consideration. Simply make your selection and deposit your money.

Once back at the lift, you can choose to go up to Mürren or down to Stechelberg.

Consider a local souvenir from an "honor store."

Past the turnaround at Im Tal is a compelling valley

For an interactive map and elevation profile, visit
https://www.plotaroute.com/route/1685238

Hike #15 – Stechelberg Loop

Start:	Hotel Stechelberg Post Bus Stop
End:	Hotel Stechelberg Post Bus Stop
Duration:	50M
Difficulty:	2
Distance:	1.7 miles/2.7 kilometers
Ascent/Descent:	515 feet ascent/492 feet descent
Type of Hike:	Loop
Transportation:	Post Bus to Stechelberg
Refreshments:	Hotel Stechelberg
WCs:	Hotel Stechelberg
Hiking Boots?	Recommended
Trekking Poles?	Optional

Many people walk the Lauterbrunnen Valley to and from Stechelberg (see Hike #2). We love that stroll and during a long visit we will do it weekly. The south end of the valley beyond Stechelberg is quiet and is the launching point for some ambitious hikes such as Tanzbödeli, which is far beyond our easy-hiker style.

Looking back on Stechelberg from the hike.

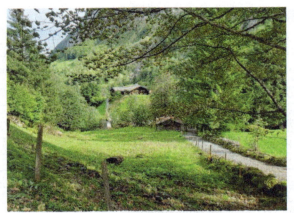
The quiet end of the valley, south of Stechelberg.

You can experience this less-visited, peaceful end of the valley in a short walk offering good valley views, a lovely rushing mountain stream, and a distant alpaca farm. We timed it for a post-hike lunch in the garden at Hotel Restaurant Stechelberg and we were not disappointed. There was a "sheep parade" while we drank our beer. Delightful.

Take the Post Bus to the Hotel Stechelberg stop. From here, proceed past the hotel bearing left at the fork which becomes more trail than road. It is a simple matter to follow this trail gently uphill passing below farms and through a small settlement, Rütti, with the *Weisse Lütschiene* bubbling below you. Take the second bridge just past Rütti. You will reach the high point of the walk at about .7 miles.

After the bridge, take the sharp right onto a road, now downhill, and following the undulating road back to Stechelberg enjoying valley views. Be certain to look across the valley for the alpaca farm in the distance.

Return to Lauterbrunnen by Post Bus, but stop at the hotel for refreshments, first, and enjoy the lovely garden.

Weisse Lütschiene

For an interactive map and elevation profile, visit
https://www.plotaroute.com/route/1702780

Hike #16 – Lauterbrunnen to Zweilütschinen

Start:	Lauterbrunnen
End:	Zweilütschinen
Duration:	1H20M
Difficulty:	2
Distance:	2.7 miles/4.3 kilometers
Ascent/Descent:	98 feet ascent/557 feet descent
Type of Hike:	One-Way
Transportation:	Berner Oberland Bahn (BOB)
Refreshments:	Lauterbrunnen
WCs:	Lauterbrunnen and Zweilütshinen
Hiking Boots?	Not required
Trekking Poles?	Not required

This is a nice option for a cloudy or even drizzly day, or on a day when you don't want a lot of strenuous ascent/descent. The start is a bit steep downhill but easy enough. Bring trekking sticks if you are at all unsure of your footing. Once down by the river it is mostly flat. We rated this hike as a "2" only because of the stairs, which would be the toughest portion with a stroller. You can easily take the walk in the opposite direction as well, either as a one-way return to Lauterbrunnen or as a roundtrip.

Excellent signage as we find everywhere we hike in the region.

From the Lauterbrunnen Bahnhof, walk on the lower level past track 4. Turn left and follow the yellow *Wanderweg* signs down a set of stairs on your right to a parking lot. Turn left and cross the parking lot to a small road, again marked with a yellow sign. Follow the path above the river to a set of rough stairs. This is the most difficult part of the walk as the stairs are roughhewn. Although there are rough handrails, we liked having our sticks for stability here. Take small children by the hand.

From here the path is mostly flat with some undulation. It is easy to follow. There are occasional houses, many fields with cows, and frequently there are views of the river and the train as it passes.

Arrive in Zweilütschinen where you can take a train back to Lauterbrunnen or on to Wilderswil or Interlaken. You can also continue to hike to Wilderswil using **Hike #17**.

Hike along the rushing river.

For an interactive map and elevation profile, visit
https://www.plotaroute.com/route/2097783

Hike #17 – Zweilütschinen to Wilderswil

Start:	Zweilütschinen
End:	Wilderswil
Duration:	1H30M
Difficulty:	1
Distance:	3.1 miles/5.0 kilometers
Ascent/Descent:	278 feet ascent/501 feet descent
Type of Hike:	One-Way
Transportation:	Berner Oberland Bahn (BOB)
Refreshments:	Wilderswil
WCs:	Wilderswil
Hiking Boots?	Not required
Trekking Poles?	Not required

This is a great walk for a cloudy or even drizzly day, or on a day when you don't want a lot of strenuous ascent/descent. The walk is on a road that is much-used by cyclists and for portions of the walk the Berner Oberland Bahn (BOB) is in view as it conveys passengers between Interlaken and Lauterbrunnen.

Take the BOB to Zweilütschinen. This is where the train route splits and travelers coming from Lauterbrunnen change trains to go to Grindelwald and those coming from Interlaken need to be certain they are in the correct section of the train for their destination as the train actually splits in two parts, heading for the respective termination points.

Once off the train, head across the tracks – mind the trains – toward the large metal building and turn left, following the trail direction sign "Wanderweg" and further signs which point to Wilderswil. Follow this road with some undulation until the final descent to Wilderswil, passing small farms and holdings. Keep an eye out for the BOB and some excellent photo opportunities. At two miles you pass through the settlement of Gsteigwiler after which the final descent begins.

This "trail" is mostly a road used by cyclists and locals.

At Wildersil, cross the covered bridge and simply follow the street on the left to the train station. Wilderswil is a cute little town worth exploring as well. There are castle ruins a 20-minute walk from the train station, several restaurants, and (most importantly) a grocery store that is open on Sundays.

Return to Lauterbrunnen (or Interlaken) via the BOB from Wilderswil station.

N.B. A nice outing is to arrive at lunchtime. **Luca Piccante** is a fine Italian restaurant in Wilderswil that we recommend. Reservations suggested as it is very busy even at lunch. From the restaurant, follow your smartphone directions to the castle ruins, **Burg Unspunnen**. From the ruins, it is a 23 minute walk to Interlaken West or about 40 minutes to Interlaken Ost. Work off that pizza!

Looking down on Wilderswil from the path.

The Berner Oberland Bahn, aka, BOB.

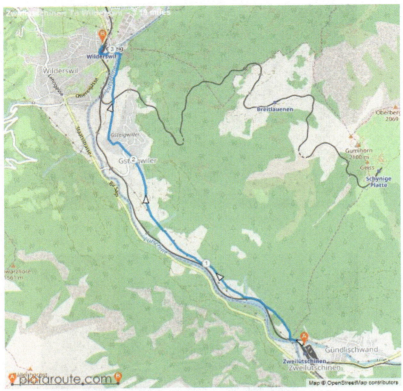

For an interactive map and elevation profile, visit
https://www.plotaroute.com/route/1684249

Hike #18 – Oeschinensee Trail to Lake

Start:	Oeschinensee Mountain Lift Station
End:	Oeschinensee Mountain Lift Station
Duration:	25M out/40M return
Difficulty:	2
Distance:	2.4 miles/3.8 kilometers
Ascent/Descent:	426 feet descent/426 feet ascent
Type of Hike:	Lollipop Loop
Transportation:	Gondola lift from Kandersteg Valley Station
Refreshments:	Two restaurants and a snackbar on the lakeshore
WCs:	At the restaurants and the lift station
Hiking Boots?	Not required
Trekking Poles?	Not required

The Kandersteg area has a number of easy hikes and this is an iconic must-do. It is a perfect itinerary for combining lunch with a walk as there are a couple of lovely terraces lakeside for dining.

NB: From Lauterbrunnen to Kandersteg is one hour and forty two minutes *one-way* by train, changing at Interlaken Ost and Spiez.

It is a modest walk from the center of Kandersteg to the valley lift station, however you can also take a bus if you want to save your energy for hiking. Once at the top, choose between walking to the lake or taking the Electro-Shuttle. You can also choose to walk down and return by Electro-Shuttle. The route is downhill all the way to the lake and uphill on the return.

The view from Trail #5.

Walking, you will soon come to a Y in the trail and must choose a left turn onto Trail #5 or to proceed straight ahead on Trail #4. We randomly chose Trail #4 and enjoyed our walk very much, however, Trail #5 affords a better view of the lake from above. Trail #5 has a couple of steep portions, though, that could be challenging for some people no matter the direction. These steeper portions are what led us to rate this a "2" on the easy-hiker scale. Otherwise it is quite an easy hike with a great rest stop at the lake. No matter which way you take the loop, there will be cows on the trail which adds a fun dimension.

Once at the lake you can relax at a restaurant on a terrace with a view of the lake, have a picnic, walk further along the lakeshore, rent a boat, or take a swim. For more information, please see the Kandersteg website, **bit.ly/KandInfo**.

View of the lake arriving on Trail #4.

When you have had a break at the lake and are ready to return, proceed behind the Berghaus Oschinensee to find Trail #5, leading uphill, eventually rejoining the stick of the lollipop and following it back to the gondola. The return will probably take you longer than the downhill outbound walk did.

Kandersteg

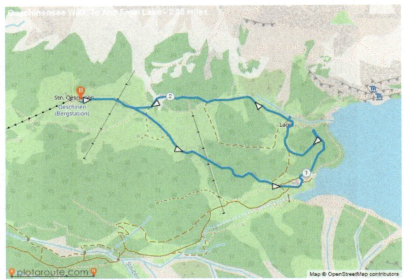

For an interactive map and elevation profile, visit
https://www.plotaroute.com/route/1686597

Hike #19 – Sunnbüel-Arvenseeli

Start:	Sunnbüel Mountain Lift Station
End:	Sunnbüel Mountain Lift Station
Duration:	2H
Difficulty:	2 to 3 depending on route choice
Distance:	3.5 Miles/5.6 Kilometers
Ascent/Descent:	439 feet ascent/439 feet descent
Type of Hike:	Lollipop
Transportation:	Bus from Kandersteg to valley lift station; Gondola to mountain station
Refreshments:	Bergrestaurant Schönbühl
WCs:	Bergrestaurant Schönbühl
Hiking Boots?	Recommended
Trekking Poles?	Recommended

On a plateau above Kandersteg, a family-friendly hike with modest elevation changes. There is a rocky part around the lakes area (optional route) that caused us to rate this a "3" on the easy-hiker scale, but otherwise it is a "2." We saw families with small children enjoying the area and Saturday lunch at the restaurant.

NB: From Lauterbrunnen to Kandersteg is one hour and forty two minutes *one-way* by train, changing at Interlaken Ost and Spiez.

Bus #241 takes you from the Kandersteg Bahnhof (it also stops at the church stop, Kandersteg Kirche) to the valley station of the gondola. Getting on at Kirche, our bus was very crowded on a Saturday morning in September having filled up with day-trippers arriving at the train station. The gondola runs frequently on an eight-minute trip to the top.

Heading straight from the lift station/restaurant/hotel, arrive at a "Y" and determine clockwise or counter-clockwise. We chose clockwise which the map reflects.

*The trail is primarily a road through a wide valley.
There are cows, in season, as this is pastureland.*

Descend gently into a broad meadow rimmed by rocky outcroppings. This is grazing land and there may be periodic and seasonal gates to pass through. Make sure to close them securely behind you. Most gates are marked with a yellow flag so you know where there is a safe place to open it and avoid any current.

At about one mile, you will pass through a wet lowland and shortly come to a farm on your right, Spittelmatte. Here there are three options:

(1) Turn into the driveway and up the small hill between the buildings towards the bench and turn left. This choice puts you on a rough trail amongst cows.
(2) Continue on the road to a trail sign for Arvenseeli that points to an open field; take the "faintly outlined" path across the field. It shortly joins the same path in choice 1.
(3) Stay on the road to the Arvenwald; it ultimately joins with same path as above but is less rocky. It misses past the two lakes (dry when there has not been rain) but passes by a third one. **This is the route shown on the map** and is a "2" on our scale.

Options 1 & 2 have some rocky footing and is what caused us to arrive at a rating of "3" for these options and suggest hiking boots and trekking poles. The trail passes through the woods to two little alpine lakes, the Arvenseeli, which were dry in the late season when we visited but reportedly are quite charming when there is water. We encountered several gates as there were cows grazing in these woods.

These cows followed us along the path until we passed through the gate, signified by the yellow tape.

Emerging from the woods, once again on an easy path, ascend passing grazing cows. Listen for the whistle of marmots as they laze in the sun. Shortly before the 3 mile point, you will start to descend coming again to the "Y." Turn left to arrive back at the restaurant and lift station.

Cows have a great view.

Chances are you will be able to do this hike in less than two hours unless you stop to take dozens of pictures as we did on this pretty fall day. Enjoy lunch (or a beverage) at the restaurant. The people are very nice and will put up with any effort you might make at speaking German.

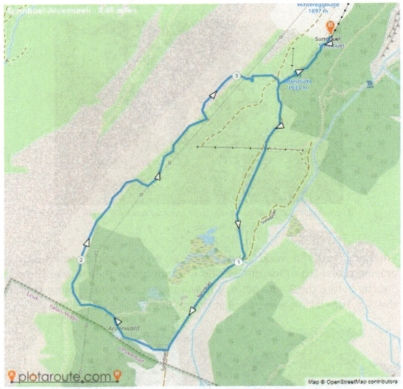

For an interactive map and elevation profile, visit
https://www.plotaroute.com/route/1792394

Hike #20 – Lötschberger Nordrampe: Kandersteg to Blausee

Start:	Kandersteg Bahnhof
End:	Blausee Naturpark
Duration:	1H30M
Difficulty:	1
Distance:	3.2 miles/5.2 kilometers
Ascent/Descent:	183 feet ascent/1059 feet descent
Type of Hike:	One-way
Transportation:	Return by bus
Refreshments:	Restaurant at Blausee
WCs:	Blausee
Hiking Boots?	Not required
Trekking Poles?	Not required

NB: From Lauterbrunnen to Kandersteg is one hour and forty two minutes *one-way* by train, changing at Interlaken Ost and Spiez.

The route is called the Lötschberger Nordrampe and runs 20 kilometers from Frutigen to Eggeschwand). Our hiking route covers only the section between Kandersteg and Blausee Naturpark (towards Frutigen). For a complete map of both the south and north ramps and the various hiking options, check with the TI in Kandersteg. You may want to build in an extension or explore other segments.

For this segment, start at the Kandersteg Bahnhof. Facing the front of the station at street level, take the Blausee trail to your right. The route begins with a level path along the river and parallel to the railroad tracks that takes you past an inactive power plant to a junction with a paved road. Turn left, going uphill (the signage is silent about the destination, but shortly you will gain confirmation from another sign). At this point the route is on roads, with some paved sections, much of it downhill, passing farms, mostly in sight of the Kander River, as well as in sight of trains. Between 2.5 and 3 miles note that the trains above you are running in a figure-8 tunnel configuration that allows them to gain and lose significant altitude in a very short distance. The diagram at Wikipedia (see **Bit.ly/WikiTunnel**) illustrates this engineering marvel.

(see **Bit.ly/WikiTunnel**)

As is often the case when walking in Switzerland, there will be cows.

Near the end of the hike you will cross over the river on a walkway (a sign directs you to Naturpark Blausee) which leads to a small, picturesque lake. This is your destination. At the time we visited in September, there was no admission fee required to enter through the "back door" from the path. Entering from the parking lot in the front requires an entry fee. This could change depending on season. The Blausee is so clear you can see tree trunks that appear to be just under the surface yet they are submerged in 12 meters of water. Information on the Blausee is on the BLS site **(see bit.ly/BlauInfo)**.

The bridge to the Blausee Naturpark.

These trees are 12 meters/39 feet underwater.

There are a café and restaurant as well as a WC at the Blausee.

When you are ready to move on or to return to Kandersteg, follow the paved path next to the lake past the Restaurant Blausee and the Blausee Café through the woods and through a parking lot to the junction with a major road. The bus stop is in front of the restaurant on your left.

For an interactive map and elevation profile, visit
https://www.plotaroute.com/route/1793500

Hike #21 – Bussalp to Bort

Start:	Bussalp Bergrestaurant
End:	Bort Lift Station
Duration:	2H15M or 1H50M
Difficulty:	2
Distance:	4.6 miles/7.5 kilometers OR 3.8 miles/6 Kilometers
Ascent/Descent:	708 feet ascent/1433 feet descent OR 643 feet ascent/1066 descent
Type of Hike:	One-way
Transportation:	Bus to Bergestaurant Bussalp; Lift from Bort to Grindelwald
Refreshments:	Bergrestaurant Bussalp; Raschthysi Hütte; Bergrestaurant Bort
WCs:	Bergrestaurant Bussalp; Raschthysi Hütte; Bergrestaurant Bort
Hiking Boots?	Recommended
Trekking Poles?	Optional

A delightful and scenic hike, the best bus ride ever, a charming trailside café, cows galore, and a convenient return by cable car. What's not to love? This is a lovely outing to explore the Grindelwald area. With an early departure, you can be in Grindelwald in time for lunch on the terrace at Bebbi's. There is an option to start the hike at Holzmattenläger, one bus stop from the top, eliminating over 300 feet of descent.

Bus 126 departs from the bus plaza near the Grindelwald train station. This is an infrequent bus so check the schedule on the SBB app and plan accordingly. The ride to the terminus at the berg restaurant takes 35 minutes. This is a thrill ride with narrow roads, incredible vistas, and lots of cows. Our driver, Francesca, had nerves of steel and impossible patience with road blocking cows. Even if you do not hike, the bus ride is worth taking.

Cows keeping an eye on hikers.

The beginning point of the hike is a bit unclear. The sign pointed down a steep slope with no obvious path so we chose to go via the road, which we recommend. As the road levels out, coming to a vehicle track across a meadow, follow the faint trail that would seem to coincide with the downhill route indicated at the top. Soon you will see a yellow hiking sign in the distance. Head toward the sign and find a very faint path through the grass that eventually leads to a bridge and a confusing sign. Proceed directly up a slight hill where you will encounter the road the bus took and further signage including the bus stop at Holzmattenläger. This sets you on the right course, the Höhenweg 1600 and a rather decent gravel road which continued in a generally downhill direction. From here there are a mix of roads, paved, graveled, and unimproved as well as true trails. **NB:** You can stay on the road all the way to Holzmattenläger and avoid the faint cross-country paths or you can shorten the hike by getting off the bus at Holzmattenläger and starting from there.

Rasthysi

Reaching Rasthysi at about 1.5 miles, a charming *hütte* for refreshment, worth a stop for coffee and locally baked pastry or lunch and a beer. There is a WC. Note this can be a busy *hütte* on a fine day as it is accessible by car and bus. If you fancy a short outing, the bus #127 (June-October only) can take you back to Grindelwald or you can start here and take an abbreviated hike to Bort.

Clear signage: Stick to the route to Bort

Continue on the route past two bus stops at Abzwergung and Nodhalten. Keep following signs to Nodhalten/Bort Station/Höhenweg 1600, passing a picnic spot and a couple of buildings at Nodhalten. The trail has a little uphill after this point but not much. Towards the end, it truly becomes a path for a while. Views are terrific and the forested sections very pleasant. Reaching Bort, there is another restaurant, WC, and a playground to enjoy, or simply board the gondola for the ride down to the valley.

The most difficult portion of this route can be avoided by starting at Holzmattenläger (the next-to-the-last bus stop) instead of Bussalp. This alternative starting point of Holzmattenläger is shown in the map below.

Views abound. This, near Bort on a fine September morning.

For an interactive map and elevation profile, visit
https://www.plotaroute.com/routecollection/8304

OTHER EXCURSIONS

A day-off from hiking offers an opportunity to explore some other venues in the Berner Oberland. Here are a few we have enjoyed.

Sulwald and Isenfluh

Above Lauterbrunnen, reached via Post Bus, is the tiny hamlet of Isenfluh. Above Isenfluh, Sulwald is even smaller. The mountain views on a clear day are extraordinary and while there is true hiking to be had, we like to simply take the tiny 8-passenger lift (pictured) – also used for cows; ask the attendant how they do that – from Isenfluh to Sulwald. We walk along the road 15 minutes to the viewpoint (*Aussichtspunkt* on the sign) then descend to Isenfluh for lunch on the terrace **Hotel Restaurant Waldrand**. Take a walk through Isenfluh – it only takes a few minutes – before you catch your return bus.

The lift runs from 7:00 to 18:15, usually every 15-minutes, and at extra cost even with your pass. The experience is worth every *pfennig*. Be sure to check the bus schedule and plan accordingly as service is infrequent.

Ballenberg, Swiss Open Air Museum

On the far side of Lake Brienz near the town of Brienz is an amazing museum. To visit **Ballenberg** is like walking across all of the cantons of Switzerland in 50 acres. See the differences between Ticino, the Valais, and the Jura. There are over 100 homes, barns, and other historic buildings from all over Switzerland. More than 50 years ago the far-sighted Swiss made a decision to protect and preserve their heritage and established Ballenberg. You might enjoy reading the history at **bit.ly/BallHist**.

Enter at the east entrance (train to Brienz, then bus #151 direct to the museum, about 1H30M) and use the (extra-cost) map/guide to enlighten your visit. In addition to historic preserved buildings, there are animals, demonstrations, and restaurants. Walk through to the west entrance where you will find the #151 bus for your return.

You are welcome to bring a picnic to enjoy in one of the many picnic areas. Entry is included in the Swiss Travel Pass and Flex Pass.

Interlaken

Interlaken is more of a city than a town and your impression may be tarnished by the busy train station and unremarkable plaza in front of it. We felt this way until we took the Rick Steves' Interlaken Walk in his Switzerland guidebook. It takes less than an hour and even on an overcast, drizzly day we enjoyed this mini tour.

If you are spending a significant length of time in the area, shopping at the Coop by the train station may be worth your while. The selection is more robust than at the little stores in Lauterbrunnen, Wengen, and Mürren. There is also a cafeteria where you can enjoy lunch at a reasonable (for Switzerland) price.

Bern

A day trip to big-city Bern is free with your Berner Oberland Regional Pass. While we would not take away from a fabulously sunny hiking opportunity to visit Bern, perhaps after a week of steady hiking or on a cold, rainy day, Bern might be the right choice. Your journey by train will take 1H20M-1H30M depending on connections.

The Schilthorn and the Jungfraujoch

Expensive, time-consuming, and unique, perhaps your must-do list includes one or both of these experiences. They are experiences, certainly, and we have visited both. I would not, after visiting, call them must-dos for active travellers.

You can enjoy the Berner Oberland fully without taking either trip. With good weather and limited time, one must decide between a spectacular hike or a crowded, expensive trip to a high mountain peak where you can shop and dine.

Schilthorn Pros and Cons

Pros:

- Site of the 1966 James Bond movie, *On Her Majesty's Secret Service*. Fun for the fan.
- Dramatic 30-minute, two-stage gondola ride, one to Birg from Mürren and the second to Piz Gloria.
- Panoramic view of the three peaks
- Skyline Walk at Birg
- Watch paragliders sail off the top to land in the valley
- In winter, watch advanced skiers flying down the mountain
- Have an expensive but good meal in the rotating restaurant

Cons:

- Price. Discounted with a Half Fare Card or Berner Oberland Regional Pass. With a Berner Oberland Regional Pass you pay half price from Mürren to Piz Gloria and return. Travel to Mürren is included in the pass.
- Time-consuming (although not as bad as the Jungfraujoch "Top of Europe" trip), about an hour transport time each way from Lauterbrunnen, plus whatever time you spend at the top, probably a total of 4 hours.

Jungfraujoch "Top of Europe" Pros and Cons

Pros:

- Nowhere like it: Highest railway station in Europe at 11,333 feet.
- An engineering marvel, a tunnel built through the Eiger more than a century ago, by Italian workers.
- An observation deck at 11,700 feet with amazing views on a clear day. Note: clear day is key. The cloud deck may be between the observation deck and the valley, obscuring everything.

- You can ski, snowboard, and go sledding on a glacier (extra cost), or you may hike an hour across the glacier (pictured below) to the Mönchsjochhütte.

Cons:

- Expensive: CHF 195 roundtrip from Lauterbrunnen, full-fare, discounts with passes. Even with a Berner Oberland Regional Pass, the additional cost is CHF 99.
- Cold: Even in summer it is cold in the train and hovers near freezing at the top and it can be windy.
- Crowded. The train is SRO at peak times.
- Time-consuming: 1H30M each way from Lauterbrunnen. Add in time at the top, and it is easy to spend 5-6 hours on this outing.

We do not want to discourage either of these trips, just establish perspective. They are not, in our opinion, "must-dos." If weather, time, or budget constraints prohibit the excursion, you will still have a magnificent time hiking in the region.

RAINY DAY IDEAS

Despite endless photographs of sunny trails and bright snowy peaks, Mother Nature also blesses Switzerland with ample rain. We are happy to report that *usually* it rains on-and-off for part of a day or a day at most but occasionally (Fall of 2022 I am thinking of you!) you may have several days in a row. All the more reason to spend as many nights as possible in the area so you are able to experience some fabulous dry days.

Should rain be in the forecast, don't fret, there are plenty of options for activity and entertainment. Here are a few of our favorites.

Hikes 2, 13, 16, & 17 do not suffer from light rain as they do not depend on views as much as higher elevation options.

Mountain Joy Riding. If you have a pass (and one of the very good reasons to have a pass is to take advantage of it on a less-than-perfect day or a day you don't want to hike), you can ride most of the day and see amazing scenery despite the weather. Here is our suggested itinerary for a Grand Tour of the Jungfrau Region.

- Board the Wengernalpbahn (train) from Lauterbrunnen to Wengen and on to Kleine Scheidegg at 2061 meters/6762 feet of altitude
- Change trains at the top and ride down to Grindelwald
- Have lunch in Grindelwald and explore the shops
- Take the BOB to Grindelwald Terminal, the base station for two fabulous lifts, the new Eiger Express and the Männlichen Gondolbahn
- Ride the Männlichen Gondelbahn to Männlichen via this amazing long cableway https://www.maennlichen.ch/en/
- Descend from Männlichen to Wengen via the cableway
- Ride the Wengernalpbahn back to Lauterbrunnen

The Berner Oberland Regional Pass is expensive but the value is there and once purchased it is a no brainer to hop on any lift or train or bus and go anywhere in the region. In 2022 when we did it, this trip would have cost CHF 134.00, but with the pass the additional out-of-pocket cost is zero. We used 1/3 of the face value of our 10-day pass in this single day and still had 9 days to do as much riding as we desire. The pass is available for 3, 4, 6, 8, and 10 day periods. There is a further discount on the pass if one buys a Swiss Half Fare Card which I also recommend. See the chapter on PASSES AND TRANSPORTATION PLANNING.

View from the Wengernalpbahn as it descends to Grindelwald.

Three Village Tour. For a we-don't-want-to-do-much day, rain or shine, one can explore the three villages of the Lauterbrunnen Valley and do some shopping. Take the train up to Wengen and walk the village, see the view by the church, and maybe stop for coffee. Coming back down to Lauterbrunnen, stop at the Tourist Information Office to see what might interest you that you haven't thought about, then walk the length of the village, perhaps past the Staubbach Falls and as far as Camping Jungfrau. You could have lunch in the village. Finally, take the lift from Lauterbrunnen to Grütschalp and the little train to Mürren, walk the village, check the shops, and descend via the Schilthornbahn to Stechelberg where you can catch the bus back to Lauterbrunnen. We left home at 10:00 and did not return until almost 16:00. It wasn't hiking but it was a nice pace, about 3 miles of walking, and a leisurely chance to look for Christmas gifts. The rain spit off and on but there was never a deluge and there were occasional sun breaks. Another good reason for the BO Regional Pass is not having to weigh the expense of jumping on trains and lifts impetuously for shopping.

Take a cruise. The excitement factor is limited but the relaxation factor is high for a two-hour cruise with lunch on the Thunersee. Rain or shine, the BLS ships sail on both Lake Thun (Thunersee) and Lake Brienz (Brienzersee). The train delivers you to Thun, a lovely city worth exploring, right next to the landing for the ships. Arrive a bit early and explore the shops along Obere Hauptgasse. After boarding the ship you can choose from a varied menu of choices from soups and salads to multi course meals or a snack. There's plenty of time for a leisurely lunch while hopping from town to town along the lake with distant peaks and nearby waterfalls in view. There are also cruises that are not meal-centric. (See https://www.bls-schiff.ch/en.) Cruises on both the Thunersee and Brienzersee are free with your Berner Oberland Regional Pass.

TRAVEL ADVICE

Trail signage is excellent. You will not get lost!

WHEN TO TRAVEL

The summer season is from May to mid-October. The other season is mid-December to roughly Easter, when skiers flock to the area. Certainly, you can visit any time but hiking in the mountains out-of-season (mid-October to early December and late March to mid-June) will be limited severely by a lift closures, muddy conditions, and possibly be snow until early June at some elevations.

Sled rental, Mürren

Winter is beautiful in the Jungfrau Region and as the Swiss embrace walking at all times of the year, some trails are groomed trails for *winter wandern*. We have hiked Grütschalp to Mürren and the North Face Trail in the winter but be certain to ask locally about conditions and by all means have sturdy winter hiking boots and trekking poles.

SAMPLE ITINERARIES

If you have 3 nights

A three-night stay allows a nice taste of the region with two full days. Spend one day on the Mürren side and the other on the Wengen side. Stay in Lauterbrunnen as it is central to both and the transportation hub. On your arrival day, at least walk up to Staubbach Falls just to enjoy the view. If you arrive early enough or are enjoying long summer daylight hours, you could easily take the Lauterbrunnen Valley Walk **(Hike #2)**. Be sure to leave time to buy your Berner Oberland Regional Passes at the train station if you don't have them yet and pick up a map.

The next morning, take the gondola to Grütschalp and embark on **Hike #1, Grütschalp to Mürren.** This is a great first day hike, not too strenuous, but very rewarding in terms of views. Also, even if it is slightly overcast there is much to enjoy. Once in Mürren, take time for a coffee break or lunch and consider taking the easy walk down to Gimmelwald then descend via gondola to Stechelberg and take the bus back to Lauterbrunnen. Long daylight hours might allow you time to go to Wengen for dinner and take the **Mönchblick Walk (Hike #9)** either before or after you eat.

On your final day, head up to Wengen and take the gondola to Männlichen for **Hike #8, Männlichen to Kleine Scheidegg.** Time your arrival for lunch at the recommended restaurant, then consider adding on **Hike #7, Kleine Scheidegg to Wengernalp.** Otherwise, take the train back to Wengen and on to Lauterbrunnen.

If you have 4 nights

Use the three-night schedule as a guide, and add in **Hike #3 First to Grosse Scheidegg** for your third day of activity. This gets you over to Grindelwald and a completely different view of the area. Have lunch before you hike at the Berggasthaus or when you return to Grindelwald. Or pack a picnic!

If you have 5 nights

Take **Hikes 1, 3, and 8** as recommended in the 3 and 4 night itineraries and add in a day trip to take a cruise on Lake Brienz, perhaps in conjunction with visiting the Ballenberg Open Air Museum or by taking **Hike #11 Giessbach Falls.** If you are devoted hikers, **Hike #6 The North Face Trail** is a great choice, too.

If you have 7 nights

Lucky you and great decision to spend a week in this incredible area! Add in any hikes that appeal to you but by all means, get over to the Ballenberg Open Air Museum.

It seldom rains all day. If there is rain during your stay, check with the locals on expectations for clearing. A gray and wet morning might turn into a sunny and delightful afternoon, so take heart! We've enjoyed **Hike #2 Lauterbrunnen Valley Walk** on a rainy day, and Trümmelbach Falls is a great rainy day option as well.

Coming into Kleine Scheidegg on the hike from Männlichen

HOW TO ARRIVE

The Berner Oberland Bahn – BOB – in the Lauterbrunnen Station.

The Swiss make transportation sing! There is little need for a car so abandon those pre-conceived ideas that a car is more convenient or offers flexibility, especially for short stays. A vehicle will sit in the garage – for a fee – during your entire visit. The mountain towns of Mürren and Wengen are car-free.

Inevitably you will take a train to Interlaken Ost on your way to Lauterbrunnen. You might get there by changing trains at Spiez (a delightful lakeside town) or Thun (beautiful castles). No matter, Interlaken Ost is the gateway to the Lauterbrunnen Valley and you will board the BOB – the Berner Oberland Bahn – every time you travel between the two towns.

Once in Lauterbrunnen if you are staying in Wengen, cross the platform to take the Wengneralpbahn for a 20-minute ride to the village. If you are staying in Mürren, you have two choices of route. You might ask your hotel which they recommend.

1. From the Lauterbrunnen train station, take the underpass or walk across the street to the Grütschalp gondola lift. Ride the lift to the top of the cliff and transfer to the little mountain train that will take you to Mürren in 14 minutes.
2. From the Lauterbrunnen train station, take the underpass or walk across the street to the Post Bus Stop, right in front of the Von Allmen Café and Bakery. Ride the bus to the Schilthornbahn station near Stechelberg for the two-stage gondola to Mürren.

Each of the villages is highly walkable although if you have a lot of luggage you might ask your lodging establishment if they have a transfer service.

PASSES and TRANSPORTATION PLANNING

The array of passes in Switzerland is truly mind-numbing. We have, over many trips, come up with a combination that works for us, which I confirm by running a spreadsheet every trip to estimate total costs and possible savings so I can select the best combination of passes. Above all take this to heart: transportation in Switzerland is expensive. Hiking is free but getting to-and-from is not. The Swiss transportation system is top notch and you will pay for the convenience, efficiency, and cleanliness.

The Swiss Travel Pass (STP) is extremely convenient, offers unlimited travel in the country, and comes in 3, 4, 6, 8 or 15 *consecutive* day versions. It covers virtually all train, bus, and boat transportation in the country. Transport into the mountains (by cable car, funicular, cogwheel train, etc.) is discounted. It is great if you are going to do a lot of train, bus, and boat travel throughout the country day-after-day, but you'll be paying additionally for mountain transport. See **bit.ly/STPInfo** for details.

The Swiss Travel Pass Flex (FLEX) is also very convenient and offers unlimited travel for 3, 4, 6, 8 or 15 days *within one month*. You decide which days to use it. As with the STP, cable cars, cogwheel trains, and funiculars are discounted by 50%. We like this pass when we are visiting several locations throughout Switzerland. If you are staying more than 15 days, it may serve you to have a Half Fare Card in addition. See **bit.ly/FlexInfo** for details.

The Swiss Half Fare Card (HFC) provides a 50% discount on every form of transportation in Switzerland: Trains, buses, boats, lifts. It also provides a discount on some other passes you may buy, such as the Berner Oberland Regional Pass. We like this pass when we are also visiting a location outside of the Berner Oberland on the same trip and have been known to make full use of a FLEX pass, HFC, and Berner Oberland Regional Pass in a 3-week trip. See **bit.ly/HFCInfo** for details.

Berner Oberland Regional Pass is a terrific choice for those spending a significant amount of time riding mountain trains and lifts in the Berner Oberland. With one ticket (available in 3, 4, 6, 8, or 10-day versions) you have unlimited riding on all trains, lifts, boats, and buses in the Berner Oberland with a few exceptions. There is an extra charge for the lift to the Schilthorn and Jungfraujoch. Check the map on this page **bit.ly/validitymap** (download the PDF for easy reference) to see how many routes are fully covered by the pass. We enjoy the freedom of this pass if we simply want to pop into Interlaken to shop, go up to Wengen for dinner, ride the Post Bus from the train station to our lodging when carrying groceries, or joy ride up to Kleine Scheidegg and over to Grindelwald just for the view. Passes for children are at a significant reduction. See **bit.ly/BOPRegInfo** for more details.

Note validity changes *slightly* every year in our experience, so be certain to consult the newest information before you depart.

Guidelines for selecting the right passes

- How many locations you will visit in Switzerland (Luzern, Zermatt, and Lauterbrunnen in 2 weeks versus Lauterbrunnen for 4 nights) would likely justify different passes or a different combination of passes.

- Are your travel days consecutive or spread out over several weeks?

- Will you hike every day? If so, a pass that covers the most lifts makes sense.

- Which lifts and trains are required for the hikes you plan to take? Assume good weather and that your plans will work out!

MySwissAlps has a step-by-step planner **(see bit.ly/choosepass)**. On this page you will see a downloadable Excel Spreadsheet in a zip file that *might* be helpful in calculating your options. I like to make my own spreadsheet.

We have a mantra: "Just buy the pass" and don't worry too much about the cheapest option. The convenience and ability to be impetuous (lunch on a mountain top anyone?) is hard to beat.

Transportation Planning

Swiss transportation options are interconnected seamlessly. In other countries, you need to look at different bus schedules for various cities and towns as well as multiple rail services, not to mention disparate mountain lift systems. In Switzerland all forms are coordinated and you can research every single trip you wish to take at **www.sbb.ch/en**, the Swiss national railway company. We recommend familiarizing yourself with SBB's features while planning your trip.

It is generally not necessary to buy tickets in advance, nor would you want to if you will be using a pass. Just show up at the station and buy your ticket as needed, or simply get on the train (or bus) with a valid pass.

An exception in which advance purchase is helpful is when traveling to or from another country. For example, traveling from Kandersteg to Paris, a walk-up second class ticket purchased with a Half Fare Card is CHF 229.50, but an advanced purchase, non-refundable ticket can be a low as CHF 64.50 and you will have reserved seats where available.

Before you travel, download the **SBB app** to your smartphone (available for Android and iPhone). It is <u>extremely</u> useful on-the-fly and you can even purchase tickets through the app.

The personnel in the SBB offices are endlessly helpful and will come to your assistance if questions arise.

Stay in Touch

Facebook: Project Easy Hiker

Website: www.ProjectEasyHiker.com

Travel Blog: www.Girovaga.com

Made in the USA
Coppell, TX
14 April 2024

31278620R00075